FONTAINEBLEAU

TRUE ABODE OF KINGS AND PALACE OF THE AGES

Editor-in-chief: Xavier Salmon
Heritage and Collection Director, Palace of Fontainebleau

Château
de Fontainebleau

Texts by:

Xavier Salmon, Chief Curator and Heritage and Collection Director ("A lesson in history, architecture and taste"; the State Apartments, from the White Salon to the Council Chamber; the Trinity Chapel).

Christophe Beyeler (The Emperor's Inner Apartment), Valérie Carpentier (the Hunt Apartment, the Furniture Gallery, the Chinese Museum, the Lacquer Salon, the Theatre and the gardens), Vincent Cochet (the State Apartments from the Saint Louis Rooms to Diana's Gallery, the Pope's or Queens Mothers' Apartment), Vincent Droguet (the State Apartments from the Splendour Gallery to the Rotunda); and Isabelle Tamisier-Vétois (the Small Apartments of the Emperor and the Empress, the Guest Apartment). The authors are curators at the Palace of Fontainebleau.

The captions for the illustrations run
from top to bottom and from left to right

Cover:
top: detail of the cabinet commemorating
the marriage of the Duke of Orleans,
eldest son of King Louis-Philippe, to Helen
of Mecklenburg-Schwerin.
bottom: aerial view of the Palace
of Fontainebleau.

pp 4-5: main entrance and the Horseshoe
Staircase wing

ISBN : 978-2-85495-443-2
© Éditions Artlys, Paris, 2011
7, rue Biscornet 75012 Paris
www.artlys.fr

A lesson in history, architecture and taste

Averitable mosaic of additions and transformations embracing many reigns from the Middle Ages to the fall of the Second Empire in 1870, the Palace of Fontainebleau seems to lack, at first glance, the reassuring unity we like to associate with a particular sovereign or period. Yet it was this historical density that led Napoleon Bonaparte to pronounce it "the true abode of kings and the palace of the ages."

THE MEDIEVAL PALACE

Fortified and ringed with moats, the first palace owed its existence to the surrounding forest, a rich source of game and spring water. Attested since 1137, it was home to Louis VII the Young – Saint Louis – who in 1259 built a Trinitarian monastery whose monks would oversee a hospital, and Philip the Fair, who was born and died there. All of them had a passion for hunting in the surrounding countryside.

The Oval Courtyard: column capitals from the reign of François I

THE RENAISSANCE PALACE

Following the embellishments ordered by Isabeau of Bavaria in the 15th century, François I began the first of the building works that gave the building the appearance it has today. A new residence was raised on the foundations of the medieval castle, whose immense square "donjon" or keep was retained. On the forest side to the south, the Golden Gate, a monumental entrance in the Italian style, gave access to the new palace. In the courtyard an equally monumental staircase known as the Serlio Portico led

Left-hand page:
The medieval donjon in the Oval Courtyard.
The Golden Gate.
The "Serlio Portico" in the Oval Courtyard.
View from the Carp Pool: the Fine Fireplace wing, the apse of Saint Saturnin.
Chapel and Henri IV's quarters.

The Pine Grotto: Giant sculpted in the rustic manner

The Horseshoe Staircase

up to the apartments on the north side. To the west, the François I Gallery was constructed in 1528 to allow the king direct access from his bedchamber on the first floor of the donjon to Trinity Chapel. The gallery was decorated between 1533 and 1539 by the Florentine artist Giovanni Battista di Jacopo, known as Il Rosso Fiorentino ("The Red Florentine"), with a remarkable series of frescoes glorifying the king. For the first time in France interior design combined wall paintings, stucco frames in very high relief, and sculptured wainscoting, the work of Scibec da Carpi. One of the contributors to this first major project was Bologna-born Francesco Primaticcio, but it is not known if this was before or after the death of Il Rosso in 1540. The new aesthetic code brought to France by the two masters soon influenced many other painters, sculptors and craftsmen, and gave rise to what art historians now call the First School of Fontainebleau. A second phase of works began around 1540 when an enclosed lower courtyard was created to the east on land acquired from the Trinitarians: on the west side was the Ministers' Wing, on the east side the Ferrara Wing, and on the south side the Ulysses Gallery, whose decoration was entrusted to Primaticcio and his assistants. The gardens surrounding the new palace were dotted with pavilions like the Pine Grotto, whose statues of Atlas were sculpted *alla rustica*, in sandstone left with a deliberately rough finish.

During the period 1547-1559, Henri II set about finishing what his father had begun. The architect Philibert Delorme, newly in charge of the works, continued the construction of the east wing of the lower courtyard – the future White Horse Courtyard – and added an initial horseshoe staircase. On the Oval Courtyard, François I's recessed balcony was turned into a ballroom with a coffered ceiling. On the Fountain Courtyard with its Carp Pool, the Stoves Pavilion housed the king's apartment. Meanwhile decoration of the Ulysses Gallery was going ahead, as was that of the Ballroom, directed by Nicolò dell'Abate.

The Fine Fireplace Wing, built to plans by Primaticcio

The former moat, dug in 1565 for Catherine de' Medici, between the Princes' Wing and Henri IV's quarters

Between 1565-70, Henri's widow Catherine de' Medici called Primaticcio in again, appointing him Master of the Royal Buildings. On the Fountain Courtyard he completed what is now called the Belle Cheminée ("Fine Fireplace") Wing, a classical building whose facade featured two symmetrically facing staircases. From now on the use of evenly layered cut stone was de rigueur. Catherine de' Medici also ordered the digging of a broad moat around the palace as a protective measure during the Wars of Religion.

Henri IV's quarters

The Dauphine or
Baptistery Gate

Facade of the Saint Saturnin
Chapel, built by Henri IV

HENRI IV'S PALACE

After François I, Henri IV was surely the sovereign who did most to beautify the palace. In the Oval Courtyard he extended the buildings eastwards with the Tiber and Luxembourg pavilions, and in 1601-1606 he harmonised the courtyard's facades to hide the Saint Saturnin Chapel and give the overall architecture greater unity. The wall closing off the courtyard's east side included a monumental domed gateway, known as the Dauphine Gate or Baptistery Gate. Opposite, the years 1606-1609 saw the building of the Pantry Courtyard, destined for the kitchens and the officers' accommodation. A rackets, or "real tennis", court was built between the Ministers' Wing and Diana's Garden.

Inside the royal residence, decoration on a large scale went on endlessly: the Trinity Chapel was provided with a superb ceiling decor by Martin Fréminet, while the heroic cycles painted on canvas by Ambroise Dubois and Toussaint Dubreuil were the origin of the Second School of Fontainebleau. The Fine Fireplace found its place in the wing that later took its name. The "good king" had Diana's Garden, also known as the Queen's Garden, enclosed by the Deer Gallery, the aviary and the Stag Gallery. A hanging garden was built on the Carp Pool. And on the south side, facing the ballroom and the Pantry Courtyard, was the King's Garden, later renamed the Grand Parterre, with the view eastwards following the straight line of a broad, majestic canal.

Decorative sculpture on the pediment
of the Baptistery Gate

Mask on the Baptistery Gate

In this wing: Diana's Gallery and the Stag Gallery

The Princes' Courtyard

The Louis XV Wing

The Carp Pool Pavilion

Louis XIII, who was born in the palace, carried on his father's projects, completing the decoration of the Trinity Chapel and commissioning architect Jean Androuet du Cerceau to rebuild Philibert Delorme's horseshoe staircase on the White Horse Courtyard. After his death in 1643 his widow, Anne of Austria, redecorated the apartments in the Queen Mothers' wing, built by Primaticcio on the Fountain Courtyard.

FONTAINEBLEAU DURING THE REIGNS OF LOUIS XIV, LOUIS XV AND LOUIS XVI

Of all its resident sovereigns, it was Louis XIV who spent most time at Fontainebleau, revelling in the pleasures of the hunting season – late summer to early autumn – but making only a minimal contribution to its architecture. Apart from certain interior changes – the creation of Madame de Maintenon's apartment, replacement of the Baths Apartment under the François I Gallery by the Princes' Apartments, modifications to the State Apartments, and the building by Jules Hardouin-Mansart of a wing for the Court that ran parallel to the Stag and Diana Galleries – the monarch's main concern was to have Le Nôtre and Le Vau design the Grand Parterre and remove the hanging garden on the Carp Pond. The pond was then embellished with a pavillon de plaisance built to plans by Le Vau.

Determined to provide the Court with more space and comfort, Louis XV was much more active. East of the Stag Gallery he created the Conciergerie (or Princes') Courtyard, closing it off with new wings by Jacques Gabriel and his son (1737-1738). On the White Horse Courtyard the wing containing the Ulysses Gallery was gradually demolished, to be replaced by a new building that was extended westward in stages (1738-1741, then 1773-1774) towards the Pine Grotto. This new structure was intended solely to provide more accommodation.

In 1750-1754, Ange-Jacques Gabriel demolished the Stoves Pavilion on the Fountain Courtyard and replaced it with the State Pavilion, inspired by the Palace of Versailles in the simplicity of its lines, the exclusive use of a handsome blond stone, and the arrangement of the architectural orders. Inside the palace all sorts of embellishments, transformations and adaptations to current taste were going ahead, giving Fontainebleau such remarkable interiors: the King's and the Queen's Bedchambers, for example, and the Council Chamber, with its paintings by François Boucher, Carle Vanloo, Jean-Baptiste-Marie Pierre and Alexis Peyrotte. The beginning of Louis XV's reign also saw the creation of a magnificent theatre on the first floor of the Fine Fireplace wing.

Louis XVI continued his father's mission of adding still more space. On Diana's Garden a new wing along the north side of the François I Gallery enabled creation of an Inner Apartment and rearrangement of the Small Apartments on the ground floor. This meant, however that the François I Gallery lost its double lighting, keeping only the windows opening to the south.

The State Pavilion, designed by Ange-Jacques Gabriel

Grotesque mask or "mascaron" looking onto the English Garden from the Louis XV Wing

The English Garden
Diana's Fountain

Queen Marie-Antoinette's apartment was partially redecorated: the Turkish Cabinet in 1777, and in 1786-1787 the Games Room, Bedchamber and Boudoir, all in a sumptuously Arabian style.

1786 marked the Court's last stay at Fontainebleau. With the coming of the Revolution the apartments were sacked and their furniture auctioned off, although the actual structures were spared. In 1796 the Seine-et-Marne département's Ecole Centrale engineering school took over the premises, which became the Military Academy in 1803.

NAPOLEON I AT FONTAINEBLEAU

Concerned to establish his place in tradition and maintain a lifestyle and protocol worthy of the Old Régime, Napoleon Bonaparte decided to refurnish the palace completely: rapidly for the welcoming of Pope Pius VII, who was coming to crown him Emperor at Notre Dame de Paris; then more elaborately, with the creation of luxurious suites and reorganisation of the public apartments – the king's bedchamber became the Throne Room, the only one still surviving in France with its original decoration and furniture – and the private ones, which now became the apartments of the Emperor and Empress. All this made Fontainebleau what is today one of the handsomest of all surviving examples of the Empire Style.

The White Horse Courtyard now became the Main Courtyard: the Ferrara Wing, which cut the palace off from the town to the west, was demolished and replaced with the current gate. Diana's (or The Queen's) Garden and the Pine Garden were transformed into English-style parkland under the supervision of architect Maximilien-Joseph Hurtault.

LOUIS-PHILIPPE

King Louis-Philippe, who ruled from 1830 to 1848, undertook a number of projects at Fontainebleau, not only preserving and restoring the apartments, but also increasing their level of comfort and giving them the stamp of modernity. This resulted in the redecoration in a neo-Renaissance style of the Guardroom and the Plates Gallery, as well as, in a more classical vein, the Column Room under the Ballroom. At the same period the Saint Saturnin Chapel was embellished with superb stained-glass windows produced at Sèvres to designs by Princess Marie of Orleans.

THE LAST HOURS OF AN IMPERIAL RESIDENCE: THE SECOND EMPIRE

Like Napoleon I, Napoleon III enjoyed life at Fontainebleau. During his time as emperor the court made long stays there, especially in the summer months when Paris was too hot. The apartments were refurnished to suit the taste of their new occupants. Some of the historic parts of the interior were restored, in certain cases – the Stag Gallery, for example – to their original state. Numerous guest apartments were created in the attics and mezzanines. For the Louis XV wing, architect Hector Lefuel designed a theatre using a harmonious mix of yellow and gold in the Louis XVI style. The earlier 18th century theatre was lost in the fire that razed the Fine Fireplace wing in 1856. At the request of Empress Eugénie a "Chinese museum" was created on the ground floor of the State Pavilion as a home for the presents offered by the king of Siam's ambassadors in 1861, for some of the pieces brought back after the sacking of the Summer Palace in Peking, and for works by contemporary artists Winterhalter, Cordier and Barbedienne. Next door, in the Louis XV wing, were the emperor's ultra-modern study and the empress's Lacquer Room, the last real decorative ventures.

The fall of the Second Empire in 1870 led to the palace's closure, and thus to the preservation of one of the most precious parts of France's heritage. In 1927 Fontainebleau was officially declared a National Museum.

Part of the Main Gate, by locksmith Sylvain Mignon, 1809-1810

Following double page: the palace seen from the Grand Parterre

The State Apartments

Pomp and Circumstance

A hunting residence where the Court came to live for several months at a time, Fontainebleau was nonetheless also a place where etiquette ruled supreme. Situated on the first floor and giving onto the Oval Courtyard and Diana's Garden, the State Apartments were a nest of ceremonial and protocol, where the sovereigns – although probably less so than at the Louvre, the Tuileries or Versailles – had to conform to the demands of public life. The pomp that was Fontainebleau is still readily observable, for in contrast with the other royal residences, court life continued there until 1870.

The Splendour Gallery

Reached via an antechamber ornamented with paintings of Louis XV's dogs by Jean-Baptiste Oudry, and *L'Artiste*, an 1867 stained glass window by master glassmaker Maréchal de Metz, this room was created under the Second Empire. It was originally intended to house pictures of Fontainebleau in its heyday, and still contains Boulanger's *The Baptism of Louis XIII* (1834), Millin du Perreux's *Henri IV and Sully at Fontainebleau* (1819) and Demarne and Dunouy's *Napoleon Meeting Pope Pius VII in the Forest of Fontainebleau* (1808). Pierre-Denis Martin's big *View of the Royal Residence at Fontainebleau* (1718–24), shows the castle and its grounds as they were just after the death of Louis XIV.

Preceding double page: the Throne Room, former bedchamber of the kings of France

Alexandre-Louis Millin du Perreux, *Henry IV and Sully at Fontainebleau*, 1819

Plate from the royal dinner service illustrating the birth of Philip the Fair at Fontainebleau in 1268. Sèvres manufactory

Cabinet commemorating the marriage of the Duke of Orleans, eldest son of Louis-Philippe, and Helen of Mecklenburg-Schwerin. Sèvres manufactory, 1841

The Plates Gallery

Louis-Philippe had this gallery built in 1840 on what had previously been a terrace. The lower half of the walls was inset with 120 painted plates, made at the porcelain works in Sèvres and recounting the history of Fontainebleau. Above the wainscoting and on the ceiling were paintings originally in Diana's Gallery, which was decorated by Ambroise Dubois in 1601-1606 and demolished in 1810. Made at Sèvres in 1841, the cabinet commemorates the marriage of the Duke of Orleans, eldest son of Louis-Philippe, with Duchess Helen of Mecklenburg-Schwerin.

The Plates Gallery

Door leading to the Trinity Chapel gallery. The stucco decoration is by Germain Gissey and the leaves of the door were carved by Jean Gobert

The Horseshoe Vestibule

Giving onto the Horseshoe Staircase, this room leads to the François I Gallery on the east side and the gallery of the Trinity Chapel on the north side. The doors opening onto these two spaces were sculpted by Jean Gobert in 1639, with the rest of the decor dating from Louis-Philippe's time.

The sovereigns assisted at church services from the gallery overlooking the chapel nave. The gallery was furnished with gilded wooden chairs dating from the reign of Louis XVI and the First Empire, and a carpet from the Savonnerie manufactory.

The François I Gallery:
a Renaissance icon

The gallery is on the first floor of a wing built in 1528 to link the Oval Courtyard to the Trinitarian monastery, since demolished. Initially a simple passageway, it was added to François I's apartment in 1531 and strikingly decorated by Rosso Fiorentino during the period 1533-1539. The lower part of the walls was overlaid with carved walnut wainscoting that incorporated bench seats and was embellished with the French coat of arms, the king's monogram and his emblem, the salamander. This part was the work of Italian cabinetmaker Francesco Scibec de Carpi. Above the wainscoting was a decor devised by Rosso: frescoed panels with extravagant stucco frames whose ornateness and originality were the most strikingly innovative feature of what became the emblem of the First School of Fontainebleau. Primaticcio also made a contribution as painter of the scene showing Danae, in the middle of the south wall.

François I Gallery:
two details of the stucco decoration,
and a salamander carved on the wainscoting
by Francesco Scibec de Carpi

The leaves of the François I Gallery
door were carved by Jean Gobert

The François I Gallery may be regarded today as one of the great examples of Renaissance decoration, but it has not come down to us intact: the short sides lost their Rosso paintings because of modifications carried out in the 17th and 18th centuries; the study in the middle of the north wall disappeared in 1785 with the building of a parallel wing which also led to the elimination of all the windows on that side. Nonetheless the greater part of the decor remains and was restored in 1960-1965.

Entering, we see on the window side the scenes *Ignorance Driven Out*, *The Unity of the State*, Cleobis and Biton, *The Death of Adonis*, *The Loss of Eternal Youth* and *A Battle between Centaurs and Lapiths*. Facing the windows are *A Sacrifice*, *The Royal Elephant*, *The Sacking of Catania*, *The Nymph of Fontainebleau* (painted by Jean Alaux in 1860-1861 to replace the former entrance to the study), *Ajax Shipwrecked*, *The Education of Achilles* and *Venus Frustrated*. Rich in accurate detail, the cycle of paintings paid homage to François I and his kingly virtues.

The passageway leading from the gallery to the Guardroom dates from Louis-Philippe's time. It is home to two paintings by Noël Coypel, *Vigilance* and *Equity,* and two others by Michel II Corneille, *Morning* and *Evening*. There are also two compositions featuring cupids by Damoiselet and, on the ceiling, a painting of cupids and clouds attributed to Nicolas Chaperon.

Wainscoting carved by Scibec de Carpi

Frescoes: *The Royal Elephant*, *The Abduction of Europa by Jupiter* (left) and *The Abduction of Phylira by Saturn* (right), by Rosso Florentino and his studio

Stucco ornamentation in the Francois I Gallery

The Guardroom

Created during the reign of Charles IX, the Guardroom was outside the royal apartment, with guards providing full-time protection for the royal person. Of the original decoration, dating from the 1570s, there remains a handsome beam-and-joist ceiling and a war trophy frieze attributed to Ruggiero de Ruggieri. The rest – notably the floor, which imitates the design of the ceiling in a variety of different woods – was commissioned by Louis-Philippe. The fireplace, built in 1836, includes elements from the 16th and early 17th centuries: a bust of Henri IV attributed to Mathieu Jacquet, two figures from the Fine Fireplace – also by Jacquet – and a surround by Pierre Bontemps that once graced Henri II's bedchamber. Among the items to be seen in this room are a Renaissance-style vase made at the Sèvres manufactory in 1832 to a design by Aimé Chenavard.

The Small Louis XV Salon

Michel-Ange Challes, *The Alliance of Painting and Sculpture*, 1753

The Guardroom fireplace, with reused sculptures from the reigns of Henri II and Henri IV

This room was decorated with old paintings in 1840. On the ceiling is Michel-Ange Challes' *The Alliance of Painting and Sculpture* (1753). The seven figures of the gods illustrating the months of the year are tapestry cartoons painted by François Verdier around 1685-1696. The decoration is rounded off by an *Allegorical Figure* from the French School of the 17th century.

The vestibule of Madame de Maintenon's apartment

This hallway is home to Debay's white marble *Modesty Surrendering to Cupid* (1853) and a number of paintings, among them Jean Dubois' *Bliss*, whose female figure has the features of Anne of Austria. The vestibule leads to a four-room apartment on the first floor of the Golden Gate. Occupied by Madame de Maintenon from 1686 to 1715, it was entirely refurnished under the reigns of Louis-Philippe and Napoleon III, using Ancien Régime furnishings that in many cases were of royal origin.

The Ballroom

Originally designed by François I as a loggia, this large room was completed by Henri II. The open arcades were turned into windows and the vault already under construction was replaced with a coffered ceiling. At the east end a vast fireplace was flanked by two bronze satyrs, cast by Primaticcio from old Roman statues and now replaced with copies. To the west was a musicians' gallery, as the room was mainly to be used for Court balls.

The wainscoting, ceiling and fireplace bear Henri II's monogram, his crescent-moon emblem and his Latin motto *Donec totum impleat orbem* : "Till he replenish the whole world." Beginning in 1552, the walls, pillars and the undersides of the arches were frescoed with mythological figures and scenes by Nicolò dell'Abate, who worked from drawings by Primaticcio. On entering and looking along the spandrels of the arches on the garden side, we see *The Harvest*, *Vulcan Forging Arms for Cupid at Venus' Request*, *Phaeton Begging the Sun to Let Him Drive His Chariot*, and *Jupiter and Mercury Visiting Philemon and Baucis*. On the Oval Courtyard side are *The Feast of Bacchus*, *Apollo and the Muses on Parnassus*, *The Three Graces Dancing for the Gods*, and *The Wedding Feast of Thetis and Peleus*. Above the musicians' gallery is a concert scene.

The ornamentation was restored many times, notably under Louis-Philippe, who also installed the handsome wooden floor, which replicates the design of the ceiling.

The Ballroom

Henri II's monogram

Fresco: *The Harvest*, by Nicolò dell'Abate and his studio, from a model by Primaticcio

The Saint Saturnin Chapel

The Saint Saturnin Chapel was built under François I and its keystones, ornamented with salamanders, bear the date 1546. The sanctuary, with apses to north and south, lay under a coffered vault with a lantern at its centre. In 1554, under Henri II, Philibert Delorme built the organ loft, which rests on two slender ionic marble columns. During the reign of Henri IV the coffers of the vault were given a painted decoration.

Saint Saturnin Chapel: the gallery

The King's Staircase, formerly the Bedchamber of the Duchess of Etampes

The King's Staircase, also known as the Louis XV Staircase, was built in 1748-1749 on the site of what had been the bedroom of François I's favourite, Anne de Pisseleu, Duchess of Etampes. Overseen by Ange-Jacques Gabriel, the project left intact a substantial part of the Renaissance decoration created by Primaticcio in 1541-1544.

The upper part of the walls is ornamented with alternating rectangular and oval compartments whose frescoes recount the amorous adventures of Alexander the Great. Each painting is flanked by Primaticcio's imposing, elongated female figures

The paintings on the east wall were destroyed by the 18th-century modifications, and during the reign of Louis-Philippe, they were replaced, like those on the ceiling, by works by Abel de Pujol.

The Rotunda

The Rotunda was decorated under Louis-Philippe. In the niche is the white marble *Nature* (1529), by Italian sculptor Tribolo, which was part of François I's collection.

The Saint Louis Salon

Set in the heart of the donjon, or keep, the salons had been the royal dining room and bedchamber during the 16th century. Brought together when Louis XV opened up an archway between them, they became the king's first antechamber, then the Guardroom and Officers' Room under Napoleon. Louis-Philippe had the 18th-century woodwork enhanced with gilt pasteboard and paintings from series already in the palace, notably Ambroise Dubois' *Theagenes and Chariclea* cycle, created for Marie de' Medici. Mathieu Jacquet's masterly marble relief *Henri IV on Horseback*, executed in 1600 for the fireplace in the great hall of the Primaticcio wing, was transferred to the Second Saint Louis Salon in 1836. Apart from the marquetry cartel clock embellished with Apollo's gilt bronze chariot, originally in the Château de Chantilly, the 19th-century furniture imitated that of the reign of Louis XIV, with seats covered with Savonnerie tapestry featuring bouquets of flowers on a blue background.

Mathieu Jacquet, *Henri II on Horseback.* Marble bas-relief from the Fine Fireplace, reused on the fireplace in the Second Saint Louis Room

Painted wainscoting in the Louis XIII Salon

The Louis XIII Salon

The Louis XIII Salon

After the birth within its walls of the Dauphin, the future Louis XIII, this oval room dating from the late 16th century was given wainscotings embellished with flowers and landscapes; on its upper walls and ceiling were episodes by Dubois from *Histoire éthiopique*, a much appreciated 17th-century novel. The creation of the great gates in 1757 led to the removal of four of these pictures. Acquired in 1856, the chairs were complemented by Louis XIV copies. The tortoiseshell and brass marquetry pedestal table was surrounded by the light wooden chairs and small, comfortable buttoned armchairs typical of the Second Empire.

The François I Salon

The Odyssey Cabinet: carved ebony, Paris, mid-17th century

O nce the bedchamber of Eleanor of Austria, François I's second wife, this room became the Queen's Second Antechamber in the 17th century, a dining room under the Empire, then a salon. All that remains of its Renaissance decor, however, is the stucco-ornamented fireplace with its frescoed medallion of Primaticcio's *Marriage of Venus and Adonis*. Under Louis-Philippe the inside of the fireplace was decorated with Sèvres porcelain plaques.

On the carpet woven during the Restoration for the Throne Room at the Tuileries, stands a large, gilt wood table by Cruchet, also from the Tuileries. On the walls, the Gobelins tapestries from around 1700 are based on the famous *Hunts of Maximilian*; they remind us of royal hunting visits to the palace going back to the Renaissance and the taste for luxurious wall coverings under Napoleon III. Inside the ebony "Odyssey" cupboard acquired in 1826 are engraved panels based on Primaticcio's paintings in the former Ulysses Gallery, demolished under Louis XV.

The fireplace, François I Salon

The Tapestry Salon

The Queen's Antechamber, of which only the 1731 fireplace has survived, became the Empress's First Salon. Given a coffered ceiling under Louis-Philippe, it was hung under Napoleon III with tapestries recounting the myth of Psyche and Cupid: woven in Paris around 1650, they came from Louis XIV's collection. As in the preceding salon, there are other reminders of the age of Louis XIV in the choice of the Jacob-Desmalter Boulle-style sideboards (1839) and the pedestal table (1840), with their tortoiseshell and brass marquetry. The chairs combine 17th-century lines with Beauvais tapestry featuring flowers on a pink background.

The Tapestry Salon

The Empress's Antechamber

Entered by the Queen's Staircase, the Guardroom created in 1768 leads to the suite of rooms along the Oval Courtyard and to Diana's Gallery. It has a coffered ceiling and wainscoting – installed under Louis-Philippe – covered with Gobelins tapestry of the seasons, from cartoons by Charles Lebrun. Deities are shown against backgrounds with royal residences: Fontainebleau can be seen in the *Summer* tapestry.

The Empress's Antechamber

Diana's Gallery

Reached via a vestibule and some steps, this 80-metre (260 ft) gallery was created under Henri IV as a covered walk for the queen. Dating from around 1605, the paintings by Dubois and Jean d'Hoey recount the myth of Diana, goddess of the hunt. In a ruinous state in the early 19th century, the decor was demolished – four of the paintings, however, were transferred to the Plates Gallery – and the architect Hurtault directed a new project based on the Grand Gallery at the Louvre. Divided up into compartments, the vault and the walls were intended for paintings of the great deeds of Napoleon Bonaparte, but while the setting was finished in 1815, only the purely decorative elements were added. Later Louis XVIII took advantage of the frames painted by Moench and Redouté to add scenes of the Diana myth by Blondel and Abel de Pujol. This neoclassical decor was rounded off with paintings showing the history of the French monarchy, commissioned from a host of artists working in the "troubadour" style of the period 1820-1830. With the exception of a few scenes and a large equestrian portrait of Henri IV by Mauzaisse, the paintings were removed when the gallery became a library in 1853. The globe of the world, from Napoleon's study at the Tuileries, found its place here in 1861.

The White Salon or the Queen's Small Salon

Designed in 1835 to replace the Queen's Study, for which Marie de' Medici had ordered a cycle of paintings by Ambroise Dubois recounting the story of Tancred and Clorinda, this salon remains just as Louis-Philippe planned it. In a context of Louis XV wainscoting set off by a Louis XVI fireplace and chimney, the Empire-style furniture notably includes a sofa from the Mars Salon at Saint Cloud, armchairs by Jacob Frères and chairs from the Princes' Salon (also at Saint Cloud), a standing screen made by Marcion in 1813 for Monte Cavallo, a Jacob-Desmalter console table, and a 1812 Thomire planter held up by three winged women. Used as a lounge by Louis-Philippe's wife, Queen Marie-Amélie, then turned into an informal chatting room by Empress Eugénie's ladies in waiting, this room is emblematic of the mix of styles that developed after 1830.

The Queen's Games Room or The Empress's Grand Salon

Unquestionably the handsomest surviving example of late eighteenth-century arabesque decoration in France, this salon was among the rooms completely made over for Marie-Antoinette in 1786. Working from plans by architect Pierre Rousseau, Michel-Hubert Bourgeois and Jacques-Louis-François Touzé painted the large wall panels and the beading with grisaille and monochrome compositions of twining plants, women in flowing robes, female dancers, mermaids, torches and vases, together with cameo-like treatments of subjects from antiquity. The same decorative scheme was applied in gilt to the mahogany doors. Over the doors were female sphinxes, traceries and caducei modelled in plaster by Rousseau's brother-in-law Philippe-Laurent Roland, with paintings of sacrifices to Minerva by Joseph-Piat Sauvage. On the ceiling Jean-Simon Berthélemy portrayed the Muses being crowned by Minerva.

This room is now furnished in the First Empire style which, in line with the etiquette re-established by Napoleon I, comprised two Jacob Frères armchairs for the Emperor and Empress; chairs by the same cabinetmakers for the princesses; and, for the ladies, stools and X-shaped folding chairs by Jacob Frères and Jacob-Desmalter. Covered with gold-trimmed green velvet, these furnishings are complemented by alternating green and white taffeta curtains, Jacob-Desmalter console tables, a Boulard and Rode screen, a porcelain pedestal table painted by Georget from designs by architect Alexandre Théodore Brongniart, candelabras, flambeaus and Sèvres vases; the result is a room with exactly the atmosphere it had when used by the Empress as her Grand Salon.

Joseph-Piat Sauvage, *Sacrifice to Mercury*, trompe l'oeil overdoor

Arabesque wall decoration by Michel-Hubert Bourgeois and Jacques-Louis-François Touzé

Detail: the wall covering
made by Gaudin and Savournin
in Lyon towards the end
of the Ancien Régime was rewoven
and re-embroidered
between 1968 and 1986

The bed made for Marie-Antoinette
by Sené and Laurent in 1787,
under the direction of Hauré

The Queen's and the Empress's Bedchamber

From Marie de' Medici to Empress Eugénie, all France's women sovereigns used this ceremonial bedchamber, which now offers a history of interior decoration: in the centre of a ceiling ornamented with foliate mermaids and Cupids holding festoons of flowers is the monogram of Anne of Austria – mother of Louis XIV – carved in 1644 by Paris cabinetmaker Guillaume Noyers. The decor was modernised for Maria Leszczynska, wife of Louis XV: in 1746-1747 the ceiling in the alcove, the window surrounds and the lower wainscoting were designed in the Rocaille style by Jacques Verberckt and Antoine Magnonais, together with Trouard's purple breccia fireplace and its pier glass. The doors with their arabesque motif and Sauvage's overdoors date from the time of Marie-Antoinette (1787). The bed, made by Sené and Laurent under Hauré's direction was in fact completed after the Court's last stay at Fontainebleau, and was used by Joséphine and Marie-Louise. The fabric decor, produced in Lyon towards the end of the Ancien Régime and installed in 1805, was rewoven and re-embroidered in 1968-1986 from the originals by the Prelle, Tassinari and Chatel companies in Lyon and Brocard in Paris.

The period represented by the current furniture is First Empire: the Jacob-Desmalter balustrade made for the Throne Room at the Tuileries in 1804, the sphinx armchairs attributed to Jacob Frères, the Jacob-Desmalter folding screen, console tables and standing screen, and the two Beneman chests of drawers from the next-door Games Room, installed in 1806.

Centre of the bedroom ceiling, carved in 1644 by Guillaume Noyers

Marie-Antoinette's private quarters: the Queen's Boudoir

A veritable jewel set in silver, the Boudoir was completed in 1786 as a private retreat for Marie-Antoinette. Designed, like the Games Room, by Pierre Rousseau, it combines wainscoting in the arabesque style with ornaments sculpted by Laplace and paintings by Bourgeois and Touzé; over the doors are eight sculpted plaster Muses by Roland, and the ceiling offers the Aurora and some cherubs as painted by Berthélemy. Jacques-François Dropsy's fireplace mantel is embellished with gilt bronze pieces cast and embossed by Claude-Jean Pitoin, who also designed the window fasteners. The mahogany floor bearing the queen's monogram was finished by Bernard Molitor in 1787. Of the original furniture only the rolltop desk and the hopper table, both by Jean-Henri Riesener, have survived. Decorated with mother of pearl, silver and gilt bronze, brass, and satin-finish boxwood and ebony veneer, they offer a perfect aesthetic fit with the boudoir's aura of feminine sophistication. The two armchairs are copies of the Georges Jacob model now in the Gulbenkian Museum in Lisbon. Their stool/footrest, on the other hand, is original.

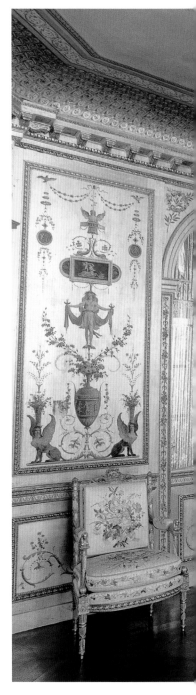

The Throne Room or the King's Former Bedchamber

Detail of the panelling carved by Verberckt and Magnonais in 1752-1754

Like the queen's bedroom, this one testifies to Fontainebleau's long history. From Henri IV to Louis XVI this was where all the sovereigns slept during their stays here. Thus we can trace back to Louis XIII most of the ceiling, part of the lower wainscoting, the pedimented doors, the bas-reliefs with their depictions of war and the medallions along the chimney wall. Verberckt and Magnonais completed the woodwork in 1752-1754, their work notably including the remarkable wainscoting on the wall facing the throne. In 1808 Napoleon I transformed the bedchamber into his Throne Room as a sign of the continuation of power. The place of the bed was now occupied by the canopy; its two ensigns topped with the monogram N, the lightning symbol and the eagle; and the dais designed by Jacob-Desmalter for Saint Cloud in 1804, from a design by Percier and Fontaine. The chair is from the Throne Room at the Tuileries. Above the fireplace, where Philippe de Champaigne's portrait of Louis XIII had been destroyed by fire in 1793, Napoleon installed his own, by Robert Lefèvre; it was removed, however, in 1834 and its place taken by the current one, a Champaigne-school portrait of Louis XIII.

Throne made by Jacob-Desmalter in 1804, to a design by Percier and Fontaine

Mid-17th century ceiling

The Council Chamber

Traversing a small room whose wainscoting is painted with pictures of birds – the king's first valet's room, where, according to tradition, the minutes were burnt once council meetings were over – we come to the Council Chamber. This room underwent ambitious redecoration in 1751-1754: the wainscoting and ceiling were renewed by Verberckt and Magnonais according to designs by Gabriel, with the five ceiling paintings by Boucher showing *The Sun Driving out the Night* and *The Four Seasons*. Carle Vanloo and Jean-Baptiste Marie Pierre painted the allegorical figures on the panels, the former using blue monochrome and the latter pink. Alexis Peyrotte was in charge of the rest of the ornamentation: floral festoons, trophies for the arts and sciences, landscapes and allegories. In 1773 the room was enlarged with a semi-rotunda giving onto the garden: the ceiling of this addition was painted with a glory of children by Lagrenée the Younger and its wainscoting was entrusted to Joseph Vernet's brother François-Gabriel. Under Napoleon I the room retained its function as Council Chamber. The chairs and folding stools by Marcion (1806) and Jacob-Desmalter (1808) enabled ministers and councillors to take their places around the emperor.

Lagrenée le Jeune, *Glory of Children*, 1773

The Emperor's Inner Apartment

Deciding that his stays at Fontainebleau warranted an apartment separate from the staterooms, in 1804 Napoleon I took over the Inner Apartment created in 1786 for Louis XVI and adapted the decoration to the taste of the times.

The Emperor's
Bedchamber

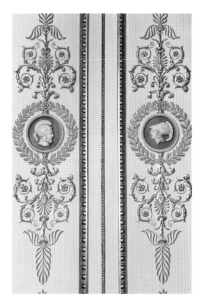

In 1808 Napoleon decided to turn the royal "powder room" – the former toilet, now decorated with Napoleonic emblems – into a bedroom. The splendid canopied bed was ornamented at its head and foot with sculpted allegories of Nobility and Glory, Justice and Plenty. Napoleon stepped out of bed onto a Sallandrouze carpet whose central motif was a Cross of the Legion of Honour, its five branches alternating with civil and military attributes: the emperor, who had worked hard to obtain the throne, wanted to make it known that those who served him well would be well rewarded. The *paumier* was an asymmetrical armchair designed expressly to let him enjoy the heat of the fireplace while inspecting the gold monochrome victories on each side. These match two candelabra placed on the sideboards, gilt bronze victories that seem to rest lightly on a cask placed on a triangular base decorated with winged lions.

Preceding double page: the Emperor's Private Salon, known as "The Abdication Room"

The Emperor's Bedchamber:
panelling carved by Laplace for Louis XV and painted by Simon-Frédéric Moench for Napoleon I

The Small Bedchamber

The emperor maintained his supremacy over his rivals and his control of Europe by an extraordinary capacity for work. In 1811 his study-library was turned into a small bedroom with an iron couch; a spiral staircase led down to the library and the nearby map room on the ground floor; here he worked on his charts, bent over a mechanical desk specially designed for him and bearing the lightning symbol as a warning to anyone thinking of challenging his absolute power.

A Roman-style ruffle runs along the underside of the cornice, and on the ceiling is *Justice Halted in Its Course by Royal Clemency* (1818), commissioned from Regnault by the Bourbons and placed here to show that the restored monarchy would not take revenge on those who had served the fallen emperor.

Jean-Baptiste Regnault, *Justice Halted in Its Course by Royal Clemency*, 1818

The Emperor's adjustable bed

Detail of the tie-backs of the curtains in the "Abdication Room": replicas of the original Louvet and Mauny designs

Thomas Allom, *Napoleon Signing the Abdication*, c. 1830

The Emperor's Bathroom

The Private Salon, known as the Abdication Room

The walls are covered with crimson brocade embellished with lyres and rosettes, and the room is furnished with similarly covered chairs, a clock from the Imperial Manufactory in Sèvres and victory-shaped candelabra by Thomire. Here the marshals of France summoned Napoleon to halt the war and relinquish power, forcing him to sign an act of abdication on the table with its bronzed pedestal.

The Passage and the Emperor's Bathroom

Decorated with views of Milan – chosen by Napoleon as the capital of his Kingdom of Italy – the passage leads to the bathroom. Attentive to personal cleanliness and a lover of hot baths with energetic rubdowns by his valet Constant, Napoleon relaxed here in a tinned copper bath lined with muslin-hemmed dimity to prevent body-metal contact. For foot-baths he had a varnished metal bucket, complete with ewer.

The passage also served as a dining room. Napoleon lunched off the English-style folding table made by Jacob-Desmalter en 1810, sipping the Chambertin wine mixed with water he was fond of, as a rule eating very quickly and rounding the meal off with a coffee, despite the Continental Blockade.

The Aides de Camp's Room

Chair with Beauvais tapestry covering

Corner cupboard made for "Mesdames", Louis XVI's aunts, at the Château de Bellevue

The Aides de Camp's Room

This was the assembly point for the emperor's aides de camp, who had to be ready day and night to transmit his orders. The wall lamps were decorated with Mercury's emblems – the caduceus and the broad-brimmed hat – and the furniture was tapestried. On the mantelpiece is a clock that matches the palace inventory of 1810: "An antique black marble clock, with a figure representing the Spirit of Study, winged flambeaus on the sides, and the front of the base ornamented with two lions and a palmette." The deposed emperor took this clock to St Helena with him on 20 April 1814.

The Emperor's Antechamber

Joseph-Marie Vien, *Hector Persuading Paris to Take up Arms*, 1783

Under the First Empire this room was decorated with four Gobelins tapestries representing Indian and animal subjects and furnished with a desk, six stools and six wooden benches, painted grey and covered with tapestry "with a sky-blue background dotted with stars and bees, and in the middle a crown surrounding an N." The room is now Second Empire, but indirectly evocative of Napoleon: neoclassical paintings – Vien's *Hector Persuading Paris to Take up Arms* (1783) and Brenet's *The Women of Rome Donating Their Jewellery to the Senate* – remind us of the Greco-Latin culture the young scholarship holder was nourished on during his studies in Autun and Brienne. In 1810 a grandfather clock with ten dials the emperor had acquired in 1806 – most likely an Italian movement in the mahogany French-made case – was in the imperial dining room in the State Apartments.

Trinity Chapel

A very long time in the making, the chapel was begun by François I and completed by Louis XIII. The actual construction process came to an end during the reign of Henri II, but the chapel remained bare until 1608, when Martin Fréminet was commissioned to paint the vault. Taking a ceiling perspective approach, he filled the compartments – first surrounded by Barthélemy Tremblay's stucco ornamentation and sculptures – with a cycle devoted to the Redemption of Mankind. Then the two masters worked together on the walls from 1613 to 1619, when Fréminet died. Work did not begin again until 1628, when Francesco Bordoni created the main altar, with its Jean Dubois painting of the Holy Trinity as Christ was being taken down from the cross. To the left of the altar were statues of Henri IV as Charlemagne and Louis XIII as Saint Louis; these were also by Dubois, as was the exquisite marble pavement.

Ornamentation in the Trinity Chapel gallery, with a cartouche showing the arms of France and the Medicis

Between 1772 and 1774 a small organ was made by François-Henry Clicquot in the galleries to the left of the altar. And in 1783 Fréminet's paintings on plaster between the high windows were replaced by fourteen scenes of the life of Christ by Taraval, Robin, Jollain, Lagrenée le Jeune, Renou, Durameau and Amédée Vanloo It was in this meticulously ornamented setting that Louis XV married Maria Leszczynska on 5 September 1725, the future Napoleon III was baptised on 4 November 1810, and Ferdinand-Philippe of Orleans, son of King Louis-Philippe, married Helen of Mecklenburg-Schwerin on 30 May 1837.

Francesco Bordoni,
Henri IV as Charlemagne
and *Louis XIII as Saint Louis,*
marble, 1628-1633

Facing page: the high altar
was completed in 1633

Private Life

The Emperor and Empress's Small Apartments

Etiquette at Fontainebleau was less strict than in the other royal residences, but the sovereigns still enjoyed breaking free of the obligations of Court life. Endlessly revamped to provide more fashionable settings, the Small Apartments were refuges where you could live as you pleased.

And they remain now almost as they were then, under the First Empire.

Situated on the ground floor of the François I wing, the Small Apartments give onto Diana's Garden and the Fountain Courtyard. This residence of the king and the royal family under the Ancien Régime was restyled in 1808-1810 for Napoleon I and Josephine. Louis XVI's studies became the Emperor's and the apartment of the royal children became the Empress's Small Apartment.

An antechamber simply furnished with painted wooden chairs leads to a first salon, where the Emperor lunched on a pedestal table. The chairs with their Beauvais tapestry covering come from the Tuileries and are similar to the originals. In the Emperor's Second Salon, also known as the Green Room, we can still see the set of elaborate gilt wood chairs made in 1810 by cabinetmaker Pierre Brion, their green velvet coverings embossed with red and purple. This ensemble is rounded off by a three-footed Jacob-Desmalter mahogany table whose gilt wood pedestal harmonises with the seating and the two big Pierre Marcion consoles, with their laurel-wreathed victory figures. These are complemented by the representation of Fame embossed on the twin firedogs. On the mantelpiece are a clock and two candelabra, originally from the imposing centrepiece made at the royal manufactory at Buen Retiro and given to Napoleon by Charles IV of Spain during their negotiations in Bayonne in April 1808. Some of the numerous parts of this diplomatic gift were later modified to suit French tastes: the clock, for example, is an assemblage now including a movement by French clockmaker Lepaute and bronzes by Thomire. On the walls are 18th-century canvases by François Boucher, Clément Belle and Joseph-Marie Vien.

Preceding double page:
The Empress's Bathroom

Part of the table centrepiece made at the Buen Retiro manufactory in Madrid around 1791 and given to Napoleon I as a gift by Charles IV of Spain in 1808

The Emperor's Second Salon

The furniture in the Emperor's bedchamber is made of gilt and bronzed wood and includes a bed, attributed to Jacob Frères, which was used by Pope Pius at the Tuileries in 1804-1805 before being brought to Fontainebleau. The chairs are from the same workshop. The canopy over the bed, by Jacob-Desmalter, is topped with ancient helmets and beribboned laurel wreaths. The furniture coverings, dating from 1858, are mottled velvet with wreaths of grapes and oleander on a white background, originally ordered from Grand Frères in Lyon in 1811. The Lepaute clock and the two candelabra adorned with vestal virgins also come from Charles IV's gift.

The Emperor's Library

The library was installed in 1808 in the former Games Room of Louis XVI's Small Apartment, of which only the panelling and overdoors by Sauvage have survived. A spiral staircase leads up to the Emperor's Inner Apartment on the first floor. The furniture comprises shelving units, a large flat desk, and a Jacob Frères stool that also serves as a step: it originally belonged to General Moreau and was acquired by the imperial administration when he was sent into exile. Jacob-Desmalter supplied the chairs with their ebony and pewter inlay, the upright writing desk, kidney table, library ladder, and the late 18th-century gilt wood sofa with its satin brocade covering. Originally intended for the Empress's guest bedroom, the sofa finally found its place here. Most of the books are still on the shelves, classified by subject in the same order as in all the imperial residences.

The bedroom of the Emperor's private secretary, Baron de Méneval, is immediately next-door to Napoleon's. It has the functional furniture that was standard for this kind of apartment, as does the one occupied by the financial secretary.

The map room, right next to Napoleon's study, was equipped with three big Jacob-Desmalter oak and mahogany tables for the emperor to peruse his maps and charts on, together with chairs and an office chair. The Louis XVI mahogany rolltop desk was installed here during the First Empire, as was the geographical clock, made by Antide Janvier for Louis XVI in 1791 and bought by the emperor in 1806. Although having no hands, the clock marks the exact time in any part of France.

The bedroom of the Baron of Méneval, the Emperor's financial secretary

Geographical clock made by Antide Janvier in 1791 and acquired by the Emperor in 1806

Rolltop desk attributed to Riesener

Next to Napoleon I's map room, the Empress's Study is still home to much of the furniture installed for Marie-Louise in 1810: writing table, letter box, embroidery frame and painting easel. The piano once belonged to Hortense de Beauharnais. The two half-moon console tables and the Jacob Frères mahogany chairs with their openwork backs, originally in the Empress's library at the Tuileries, were brought here in 1808.

A boudoir with a semicircular alcove serves as a passageway to Diana's garden. Its walls covered with green Empire silk, it is lit by a delicate, old-style alabaster and bronze swan neck lamp, made by Chaumont.

The Empress's Bedchamber

Dressing table made by Thomire in 1809 for the Empress's Bathroom

The Empress's Bedchamber, with its decor and furnishings intact, is a very feminine room, its purple and white textile finish highlighted with gold, and its bed revealing oriental inspiration. The small bedside table is decorated with poppies, the symbol of sleep, and a sleeping dog, the emblem of fidelity. The Lepaute clock is ornamented with the muses of poetry and dance. The 1809 Thomire chest of drawers reuses bronze items from an earlier Jacob Frères model which belonged to General Bonaparte and his wife when they were living in their Paris apartment on Rue Chantereine.

Now we come to the Empress's Bathroom, which has been redecorated as it originally was, using blue taffeta with a buff trim. The gilt wood Jacob-Desmalter chairs and armchairs are in the alluringly comfortable, enveloping gondola style. The sofa is on a podium and conceals a bath set in the floor. A cheval glass and toilet table round off the furnishings. The room's purpose is underscored by the bas-relief bronze Marine Venus that adorns the Thomire writing desk.

The adjoining connecting room contains Georges Jacob chairs and bergères, made in 1781-1782 for the Count of Artois's Turkish boudoir at Versailles, and moved to Fontainebleau in 1804. Their

Facing page:
The Empress's First Salon
or the Billiard Room

The Empress's Second Salon

elaborate bow and quiver decoration is unique. The Second – or Yellow – Salon still has its Empire wall coverings of purple-embroidered yellow "gros de Naples" and its gilt wood Jacob-Desmalter furnishings. An imposing Thomire and Dupasquier console table decorated with a frieze illustrating the triumph of Trajan, has its back legs made of bronze to resist the heat emerging from the vent nearby. This salon gives onto the Empress's Games Room or Billiard Room, harmoniously decorated in purple and green, and equipped with numerous chairs for players, as well as an enormous sofa. The Sèvres porcelain clock, based on a model by Chaudet, represents the Three Graces. The billiard table, however, disappeared in 1810.

The Pope's or Queen Mothers' Apartment

This is the lead-in to the State Apartments and the most lavishly decorated of all the guest suites. Emblematic of the palace's rich and varied past, its different decors are a thoroughgoing history of ongoing changes in taste. Built under François I, the wing linking the Horseshoe Pavilion and the Stoves Pavilion was taken in hand by Primaticcio to provide a new apartment for Henri II. Ultimately, however, it was occupied by his widow, Catherine de' Medici, then by Marie de' Medici and Anne of Austria – whence the designation "Queen Mothers' Wing".

At one point this apartment was lived in by the Dauphin and his wife, then by important guests, among them James II, the deposed King of England, and in 1717, Czar Peter I of Russia.

Louis XV decided to rebuild the south wing of the White Horse Courtyard. The Stoves Pavilion was demolished and its place taken by Jacques-Ange Gabriel's State Pavilion in 1754. Anne of Austria's apartment was handed on to the king's daughters: Henriette and Adelaide lived there and from 1748 onwards shared it with their sister Victoire. Summarily decorated and furnished, the State Pavilion was home to the Princes of the Line and the royal "Children of France". The wainscoting was not installed until 1784. Divided in two, Anne of Austria's apartment became that of the Count of Provence – Louis XVI's brother – and his wife.

Napoleon had the Military Academy sent elsewhere and the rooms refurnished. Pope Pius stayed here before the crowning of Napoleon as emperor in 1804, then as a captive between June 1812 and January 1814, when the apartment took on its alternative name. Louis-Philippe's eldest son, the Duke of Orleans, lived here for a time with his wife, after which the apartment was set aside for Napoleon III's cousin, the Grand Duchess of Baden.

Now incorporated into the State Apartments, this one is divided into two suites of five and six rooms, laid out symmetrically and now presented in their most recent historical state.

The Ushers' Rooms

The room allotted to the Count of Provence's Swiss Guards became Louis XV's apartment in the 19th century. Served by a staircase destroyed when the Splendour Gallery was built, it is now windowless. The velvet-covered 1860 oak chairs are a common feature of the palace's antechambers.

The Pope's Second Antechamber, transformed into the Ushers' Rooms in 1830, contains Jacob Frères painted wood furniture originally in the Luxembourg Palace during the Directory: they are covered with Beauvais tapestries of the arts and sciences, based on models by Lagrenée.

The Officers' Room and the Corner Room

Formerly an antechamber, the Officers' Room, which became the Salon of the Duchess of Orleans' ladies in waiting, has overdoors from Louis XIV's collection featuring groups of Muses by Pierre Mignard. The cartoons for the two tapestries enriched with gold thread are also by Mignard, while the Seasons from the *Galerie de Saint Cloud* tapestry, woven at the Gobelins manufactory in 1686, came to Fontainebleau in 1855.

The gilt wood chairs, some of them 17th-century and the others made by Jacob-Desmalter in 1836, accompany a Fourdinois console decorated with zephyrs and a marble-covered Souty planter of 1858.

The Corner Room, now replacing Anne of Austria's study, was the repair of the Count of Provence's noblemen and became a State Salon in the 19th century.

17th-century floral compositions have been incorporated into the 18th-century wainscoting, together with a still life with Cupid which was Joseph-Piat Sauvage's reception piece for the Academy. On the north wall the tapestry showing *Apollo among the Muses* is the fifth piece from the *Galerie de Saint Cloud* tapestry.

Chairs transferred from the Consuls' Salon at Saint Cloud in 1855 were replaced in 1859 with the ones now on show, in the Louis XV style and the work of cabinetmaker Jeanselme. Their silk covering, identical to the curtains, is ornamented with green cartouches and bouquets. Dispersed in 1889, they were reassembled in 2006-2008 around the Wasmuss table, based on models by Riesener.

Preceding double page:
Anne of Austria's Bedchamber

Jean-Louis Demarne and Alexandre-Hyacinthe Dunouy, *Napoleon Meeting Pope Pius VII in the Forest of Fontainebleau on 25 November 1808*, 1808

Autumn, wall covering in the Saint Cloud Gallery, from a design by Pierre Mignard. Gobelins manufactory

The Grand Duchess of Baden's Bedchamber

First Dressing Room, with commode
by Jean-Henri Riesener

Second Dressing Room

The Grand Duchess
of Baden's Bedchamber

U sed as a bedchamber since 1770, this room was renovated in 1837 for the Duchess of Orleans: the decor included red silk wall coverings and the gilt wood bed with fasces-shaped legs, made by Hauré and Sené for Louis XVI at Saint Cloud in 1787 and used by Napoleon at the Tuileries. Two armchairs of the same period were dismantled under the Second Empire and used by the cabinetmaker Cruchet as models for others. Cruchet also made the bed canopy, the console table and the fire guard.

Confiscated from the Council Chamber at the Château de Compiègne after the Revolution, the remarkable Stöckel and Benneman commode ornamented with military trophies inspired Fourdinois' two bedside tables (1859). The Grand Duchess of Baden, Napoleon III's cousin, was the last person to use this room.

The Dressing Rooms

N ext-door to the bedchamber, the first dressing room was decorated in the late 18th century with wainscoting whose carved trophies are echoed by the Reisener commode with a marquetry picture on its projecting central section. Acquired in 1804, along with numerous other secondhand items, the commode stands next to two gilt wood armchairs, one from the 1770s and the other a 1791 copy by Sené and Laurent for Madame Élisabeth, Louis XVI's secretary. The six console-leg Georges Jacob chairs are covered with embroidered silk and were part of the Count of Provence's furniture at the Luxembourg Palace in Paris.

This first dressing room leads to a second, which belonged to the second apartment. As a passage between the State Pavilion and the Primaticcio wing, it was initially designed for Louis XV's daughters and fitted with panelling sculpted to a design by Gabriel in 1751. It was used by the Duke of Orleans, then as a study by Stephanie of Baden. The overall decor is blue and gold: the curtains, the Directory-style chairs acquired in 1857 and the goat-headed Sèvres vases in the 18th-century manner. The tortoiseshell-and-brass marquetry commode was made by the Royal Furniture Workshops for the apartment of the Duke of Nemours, the Duke of Orleans' brother, at the Tuileries.

Anne of Austria's Bedchamber

Detail of the ceiling in Anne
of Austria's Bedchamber,
painted by Charles Errard in 1662-1664

The bed in Anne of Austria's Bedchamber,
made by the Fourdinois company in 1860

Unchanged until the time of the Duke of Orleans, this bedroom was decorated for Anne of Austria by Charles Errard and Jean Cotelle around 1660. The painted and gilt arabesques on the wainscoting are also to be seen in the compartments of the coffered ceiling. The overdoor portrait of the queen by Gilbert de Sève matches the one of Maria Teresa of Austria. Turned into a salon under the Second Empire, the room was hung with the *Triumphs of the Gods* tapestries woven at the Gobelins manufactory around 1700. Under delicate canopies, the gods are depicted among a profusion of imaginary figures and ornaments which harmonise with the painted decorations on the walls. Made of carved, gilded oak, the imposing bed and the Renaissance-style chairs were created by Fourdinois in 1859-1860 to coordinate with the existing decor, as does the Louis XIV-style Savonnerie foliate tapestry.

The State Salon

The coffered ceiling is embellished with the figures of the planets, with the sun – Apollo in His Chariot – in the centre. Sculpted in 1558 for Henri II's bedchamber in the Stoves Pavilion, it features shields bearing the French coat of arms and Anne of Austria's monogram, which means it was in the first antechamber of her apartment around 1660. This was temporarily Madame Adelaide's bedchamber in 1748, before becoming the State Salon for Louis XIII's apartment.

In 1914 the Gobelins Tapestry *The Story of Alexander the Great*, from cartoons by Charles Lebrun, replaced the *Triumphs of the Gods* tapestries installed during the Second Empire. Under the splendid crystal chandelier brought here from the Tuileries, a centre-table with a gilt wood frame matches the impressive dimensions of the room. The two console tables supported by Egyptian figures were made by the cabinetmaker Trompette and the sculptor Buteux for the presentation of objets d'art at the Royal Furniture Repository in 1787. We also see a multi-piece gilt wood drawing room setting by Jacob-Desmalter, with Beauvais tapestry coverings.

The State Salon

Detail of the State Salon ceiling, carved by Ambroise Perret in 1558

The Officers' Room
and the antechamber

Anne of Austria's former Guardroom is now the Officers'
Room and adjoining antechamber. Divided up in 1740 for the
Queen's ladies in waiting, it has kept only part of its original ceiling,
whose compartments are ornamented with allegorical celebrations
of the reign of Louis XIII, painted in gold monochrome by Charles
Errard in 1662-1664.

The Duke of Orleans' billiard room before it became the Officers'
Room, it has furnishings including a 17th century ebony cabinet.
Above the wainscoting, the *Story of Esther* tapestries woven from
designs by Charles-Antoine Coypel have been replaced by the rustic months-of-the-year subjects of the *Mois Lucas* series designed
by Lucas Cornelis.

First created with a mezzanine by Louis XV, the antechamber was
refurbished under Louis-Philippe with a Renaissance-style *carton-
pierre* ceiling. The painted embossed-leather wall hanging dates
from Napoleon III's reign and was intended to create an early-
17th century atmosphere, as was the 17th-century two-part cupboard with its doors sculpted with figures from mythology. High
Renaissance furnishings were added, among them Spanish chairs
of sculpted wood and embossed leather, adjustable wall lamps
with silver-plated reflectors, and Italian majolica vases.

NAPOLEON EMP DES FRANÇAIS

CHARAKTER UND AUFRICHTIGKEIT

The Napoleon I Museum

Fontainebleau has intimate links with Napoleon I (Napoleon Bonaparte), the emperor who transformed the palace into a sumptuous residence whose interiors still leave visitors in awe. Its long history, elaborate First Empire decoration and ornate furnishings made the palace the logical setting for the Napoleon I Museum. Since 1986, in the wing to the right of the main courtyard, the former apartments of the Prince of the Empire have been home to one of France's most precious Napoleonic collections.

Depictions of the Imperial Family

The Portrait Gallery, several of whose pictures were originally in the Family Salon in the Palace of Saint Cloud, conjures up this new dynasty, one bent on communicating its image with endless portraits: paintings commissioned from a master and copied by his assistants, or sculptured likenesses disseminated by the Banque Élisienne, which Elisa Bonaparte had founded in Carrara. In the wake of Cardinal Fesch, an uncle by marriage, and "Madame Mère", Napoleon's mother, come the other members of the family, conscientiously imitating the poses of the dynasty's founder: in colonel's uniform in Wicar's *Portrait of Joseph as King of Naples*; as Prince of France in Gérard's *Portrait of Louis as High Constable of the Empire*; as dignitary in Benevenuti's *Elisa as Grand Duchess of Tuscany*; and sculpted by Bartolini in the group *Elisa Showing a Medal of Napoleon to Her Daughter Napoléone-Elisa*. The urge for dynastic legitimacy was shared by everyone in this Corsican family, which overnight – by the grace of Napoleon I, himself depicted in 1812 as the sovereign lawgiver at the summit of his power – found itself occupying thrones all over Europe.

Ceremonies of glorification

Proclaimed "Emperor of the French" by the Senate on 18 March 1804, Napoleon was determined to have his status confirmed in the royal manner. The coronation and anointing duly took place on 2 December 1804: not in Reims, as was traditional, but in the choir of Notre Dame in Paris, and in the presence of Pope Pius VII. A few items of clothing worn at the ceremony have come down to us, together with a laurel leaf from the crown Napoleon placed on his own head. The event was immortalised by a monumental painting by Jacques Louis David and an *Album of the Coronation*. Gérard's assistants turned out portrait after portrait of the new sovereign in his imperial regalia, and of Josephine, the small Creole woman who was now empress of France. The breathtaking ceremony of December 1804 was followed in May 1805 by the coronation of Napoleon as King of Italy, in Milan.

The splendours
of the imperial table

Reviving the monarchy in his own interests, Napoleon surrounded himself with manifestations of royal power. A ceremonial
table service was an absolute necessity, and the City of Paris, at the
urging of the Prefect of the Seine département, rushed to provide
the *Grand vermeil*: 1067 pieces in all, of which various tureens,
terrine dishes, caddinets (small coffers for cutlery) and nefs
(a ship-like holders for serviettes) have survived. On its
prow the Emperor's nef bears the figure of Victory, and
on its stern those of Justice and Prudence – virtues
readily accorded at the time to someone seemingly
invincible. The Empress's nef has Charity on its prow
and the Three Graces on its stern: a virtue and a
taste for female company attributed successively to
both Josephine and Marie-Louise.
The imperial table was also adorned by sumptuous
porcelain services. Their rims embellished with a frieze
of swords, the dessert plates of the "headquarters"
service were intended to bring back pleasant memories
for the emperor: the animals of Egypt, for example, including
an *Ostrich, with a View of the Village of Nagadi*; such domestic
achievements as the *Canal de l'Ourcq*; and triumphs abroad, as in
Bringing Frederick the Great's Sword to the Invalides.

Preceding double page: King Jérôme
of Westphalia's ceremonial breastplate

After Joseph Wicar, *Joseph Napoléon,
King of Naples*, c. 1808

Pietro Benvenuti, *Elisa, Grand Duchess
of Tuscany and Her Daughter
Napoléone-Elisa*, 1809

Caron, *The Ostrich*. Plate from the emperor's
personal table service, 1808-1810

The Emperor's nef, by goldsmith
Henri Auguste, 1804

Modern recreation of Napoleon's field tent

Martin-Guillaume Biennais, silverware for Napoleon's breakfast setting, 1798-1809

Martin-Guillaume Biennais, Napoleon's travel kit (no. 4), 1809

François-Nicolas Delaistre, *Bust of Marie-Louise*

Horse-drawn gun and carriage, made for the King of Rome (Napoleon's son) by Douault-Wieland, jeweller, Paris, 1814

The King of Rome's cradle, by Pierre-Philippe Thomire, Duterme & Co and François-Honoré-Georges Jacob-Desmalter

The emperor at war

This recreation of a tent conjures up the "tent palace" that accompanied the emperor on his conquests. This large tent was in two parts: a work space with a folding table and chairs made by Jacob-Desmalter & Co., and a sleeping space equipped with a folding bed made by Desouches. The bed was guarded by Ali, the Mameluke who slept across the entrance. Ever attentive to personal hygiene, the emperor never went to war without his travel kit, bidet and enema necessities, as well as cooks able to work at the drop of a hat with a range of portable utensils that included the cauldron bearing the imperial crown and stamped "N/voyage/4".

Marie-Louise, second Empress of the French

The new empress, whom Napoleon married on 2 April 1810, was lavishly welcomed and treated with all the pomp required by her lineage and her husband's rank. It was important that her subjects should know what she looked like, so Gérard and the assistants working in his studio turned out full-length portraits, with her ceremonial mantle hanging from her shoulder and her ermine-trimmed train resting on the throne. The Imperial Manufactory at Sèvres issued several busts showing her wearing a diadem. Vivant-Denon, director of the Napoleon Museum (as the Louvre was then called) and a kind of artistic one-man band, had his own idea: taking inspiration from an ancient piece, he produced a cast and engraved silver statuette of a Roman lady with Marie-Louise's features, holding a set of brushes like a true patron of the arts.

The King of Rome: the long-awaited heir

On 20 March 1811 the son of Napoleon and Marie-Louise – the long-awaited heir – was born at the Tuileries, and duly provided with ceremonial cradles and bassinets. Appointed Governess of the Imperial Children, Madame de Montesquiou had to keep watch over the child's health, order whatever he needed, ensure his wardrobe was kept up to date and supervise him as he learned to walk. She provided the educational toys that complemented the gifts from the family and members of the Court. A model canon, a small gun with richly emblematic embellishments, uniforms and puzzles all contributed to preparing the child for the military career intended for the son of Europe's conqueror.

Unknown Fontainebleau

With its 1600 rooms, the palace includes all sorts of little-known riches, including the Princes' Apartments, the Chinese Museum and the Theatre. These patiently restored gems often have direct ties with historical figures and attest to the taste of their onetime occupants. Exploring them is a thoroughgoing lesson in history and style.

The Hunt Apartment
and the Furniture Gallery

Preceding double page:
The Stag Gallery

The Queen's Staircase

Jean-Baptiste Oudry, *Stag at Bay among the Rocks of Franchard, Forest of Fontainebleau*, 1738.

Close to the royal apartments on the first floor and giving partly onto the Oval Courtyard, the Hunt Apartment, like the similar one beneath it, served as accommodation for the Princes from the 17th to the 19th century: in the mid-18th century, for example, they were occupied by the Dauphin, Louis XV's eldest son (ground floor) and his first and second wives (first floor). The name of the apartment is a reference firstly to the Duke of Angoulême, son of Charles X, who frequently came to hunt under the Restoration; but mainly to the famed cartoons for the *Louis XV Out Hunting* tapestries, painted by Jean-Baptiste Oudry and, like those on the nearby Queen's Staircase, in place since Louis-Philippe's time.

The last occupant of the first-floor apartment was the Prince Imperial, son of Napoleon III, between 1859-1868. His salon and the bedchamber that is home to Oudry's large *Stag at Bay among the Rocks of Franchard in the Forest of Fontainebleau* (1738) have been restored to their Second Empire state.

Down the years, unfortunately, the ground-floor apartment has lost its historic furnishings, with the sole exception of a little blue boudoir. Since 2009 the Furniture Gallery has offered visitors a selection of furnishings from the palace, previously in storage and representing specific historic periods. In the gallery's first room are a number of major Ancien Régime pieces, some by René-Antoine Gaudreaus, the famed cabinetmaker of Louis XV's reign. Other rooms present items from the Directory and Empire periods. The palace was entirely refurnished by Napoleon and has retained significant examples from his time, some of them by Jacob-Desmalter, the imperial cabinetmaker. In the last rooms are furnishings created during the reigns of Louis-Philippe and Napoleon III.

The Stag Gallery

O ne of Henri IV's projects, the gallery was decorated around 1600 with oblique views of the forests and royal residences, and antlers from stags hunted in the vicinity. Louis Poisson's painted decoration suffered in the 18th century when the gallery was divided up at the end of Louis XV's and Louis XVI's reigns to create new apartments for the royal children.

In 1860 Napoleon III demolished the internal partitions and restored the gallery to its initial dimensions. This led to the discovery of the original decoration, which was then restored to the condition in which we see it today.

Jean-Baptiste Oudry, *Deformed Antler*, 1741

Primaticcio, *Laocoon*, bronze commissioned by François I for Fontainebleau, now in the Stag Gallery

Trophy in the Stag Gallery

The Chinese Museum and the Empress's Salons

The Chinese Museum Salon

Cloisonné enamel Chinese monster, Qianlong period, 1736-1795

The Chinese Museum was created in 1863 on the ground floor of the State Pavilion, near the pool, in response to Empress Eugénie's need for a space for her personal collection of Oriental items. These came from the spoils of the Franco-English punitive expedition to China in 1860, which culminated in the sack of the Summer Palace in Peking; diplomatic gifts from the Siamese embassy, received in 1861; and various acquisitions.

In the antechamber are reproductions of two royal palanquins, a gift from the Siamese embassy: one is the king's and the other, with curtains, is the queen's. The two elaborately furnished salons that follow are decorated with Second Empire sculptures by Charles Cordier and Pierre-Alexandre Schoenewerk, and exquisite Asian and European items. The billiard tables and piano signal the recreational interests of the select group that surrounded the empress here.

Through a broad arch we enter the Chinese Museum itself: walls entirely covered with black or gold lacquered panels from 18th century screens, Chinese tapestries on the ceiling, and specially designed display cabinets. Some of the pieces on show – the big chandelier, for example – were made by goldsmith Ferdinand Barbedienne from existing Chinese objects. At the far end of the museum the spectacular gilded Tibetan stupa with its statuette of Buddha comes from a temple in the Summer Palace. The focal point of the large display cabinet is a copy of the crown of the Kings of Siam, offered as a gift to Napoleon III.

The Lacquer Salon

This was the last venture in decoration undertaken under the Second Empire at Fontainebleau. On the ground floor of the Louis XV wing, near the study created for Napoleon III in 1864, the empress had her own study laid out in 1868, and decorated it, like the Chinese Museum and the adjoining rooms, in the Asian style. This exquisite room is embellished with painted lacquer panels, silk, and small furnishings and other objects from Asia.

Chinese ewers and their cloisonné enamel gold basin, 18th century, Chinese Museum

Replica of the royal crown of Siam, given to Napoleon as a gift, Chinese Museum

Chinese lacquer work in the empress's study

The Theatre

Views of the imperial theatre: the stage, the stalls and the dress circle

From the Ancien Régime to the fall of the Second Empire, entertainment was an important part of Court life at Fontainebleau. In the 18th century a theatre had been created in the Fine Fireplace wing, but it was destroyed by fire in 1856.

Napoleon III, however, had already undertaken the building of a new theatre in the Second Empire style in the west part of the Louis XV wing. The 400-seat theatre – stalls, two balconies and an entire level of latticed boxes – was built by architect Hector Lefuel in 1854-1857, in a highly ornate neo-Louis XVI style drawing on the Queen's Theatre at Versailles. The theatre itself, together with the adjoining salons and their furnishings, silks and lustrous carpets, and the stage sets, add up to a Second Empire setting still in a remarkable state of preservation.

The Carp Pool
and the English garden

S tocked with carp since the reign of Henri IV, the pool was once used by members of the court for outings in little boats. The small octagonal Pool Pavilion in the middle was commissioned by Louis XIV and rebuilt by Napoleon with the paintings inside by Moench.

The adjoining English garden is on the site of François I's Pine Garden, done away with by Louis XIV. The Pine Grotto on the ground floor of the pavilion at the end of the Louis XV is France's first artificial grotto and the sole remnant of François I's projects.

The garden took on its present appearance in 1811, with the creation of an artificial river and rocks. Near the Louis XV Wing two bronze 17th-century statues based on ancient models have been in place since the same period: The *Borghese Gladiator* and *the Dying Gladiator*.

View of the Louis XV Wing
from the English Garden

The Carp Pool

The Grand Parterre and the view towards the canal

L The Grand Parterre testifies to the changes the gardens underwent under Louis XIV. Initially a variant on the knot garden, this 14-hectare (35-acre) parterre designed by Le Nôtre and Le Vau in 1660-1664 is the largest in Europe, and occupies the site of François I's "Great Garden", itself modified by Henri IV.

The fountain installed in the central pool by Louis XIV was replaced with a different one in 1817; the round pool is home to a 1988 moulded reproduction of *The Tiber* – the ancient statue now in the Louvre – that harks back to the 16th-century bronze which once stood there.

Looking towards the Grand Canal, we see Mathieu Lespagnandel's Sphinxes (1664) near the balustrade. Beyond, on the lower level, is the cascade pool, created under Louis XIV, then rebuilt and ornamented with statues in the 19th century.

Sphinx by Mathieu Lespagnandel, 1664

The Tiber Pool

View of the Grand Canal from the Grand Parterre

The fountain in the main pool, Grand Parterre

Preceding double page:
Aerial view of the Palace of
Fontainebleau and its gardens

Photo credits:

Pascal Crapet: cover (bottom), pp. 8b; Sophie Lloyd: p. 21t, 24t, 25, 34b, 40b right, 44t, 50, 51, 60b, 62t, 62b, 70t, 70b, 80, 83b, 87t, 87b, 94-95; RMN/Daniel Arnaudet: pp. 20t, 54b; RMN/Daniel Arnaudet/Jean Schormans: pp. 63c, 76c; RMN/Gérard Blot: cover, pp. 4-5, 6t left, 6t right, 10c, 13t, 14t, 14b, 15, 18, 20b, 20c, 23b, 26, 27, 28, 31b, 32t, 40t, 41, 42, 43, 44b, 47, 53t left, 54t right, 55, 58-59, 63b, 64b, 69b, 71b, 72, 74-75, 76t, 78b, 79b left, 79b right, 82t, 82b, 83t left, 83t right, 84t, 84b, 85h, 85c, 86b, 90, 91b, 92t left, 92t right; RMN/J. Derenne: p. 38h; RMN/All rights reserved: p. 68; RMN/Georges Fessy: pp. 21b, 22t, 39b right, 45, 71t, 86t right; RMN/Jean-Pierre Lagiewski: pp. 10c, 16-17, 24b, 31t, 32b, 34t, 35b, 37, 39t, 40b left, 46, 51b, 52b, 53t right, 53b, 54c, 54 left, 56 left, 56 right, 60t, 63t, 77t, 77b, 78t, 78c, 79t; RMN/Jean Schormans: p. 38; Fondation BNP Paribas/Hugo Maertens: pp. 29b, 30, 33, 35t, 39b left, 48, 52t, 57, 61, 64t, 65t, 65b, 66, 73, 85b left, 85b right, 86t left, 91t, 92b; Xavier Salmon: pp. 6b, 7, 8h, 9t, 9b, 10t, 10b, 11 (all three), 12 (all three), 13b, 22 (three bottom), 29t, 70c, 88-89, 93.

Artlys Publishers

General editor: Karine Barou
Graphic design: Valérie Gautier
Layout: Catherine Enault
Production: Pierre Kegels
English translation: John Tittensor

Photoengraving: Jouve (Saran)
Printing: Edicolor Print (Cesson-Sévigné)

Colophon: 18 March 2015
Registration of copyright: April 2015